RHAPSODY ROAD

Ravi Shankar Etteth is a writer, editor, graphic designer and political cartoonist. In a career spanning forty years, he has worked with and headed editorial at some of the biggest media groups in the country, among them *The New Indian Express, The Sunday Standard, India Today,* Media Transasia, The Observer Group, while launching six news channels and a lifestyle channel on television.

He is a best-selling author with several critically acclaimed books to his name. These include *The Tiger by the River, The Village of the Widows, The Book of Shiva, The Brahmin,* biographies of Pawan Chamling and Naveen Patnaik, travelogues and books on art.

He lives in Delhi with his three dogs Django, Hyder and Suki.

RHAPSODY ROAD

POEMS

RAVI SHANKAR ETTETH

Om Books International

First published in 2025 by

Om Books International

Corporate & Editorial Office
A-12, Sector 64, Noida 201 301
Uttar Pradesh, India
Phone: +91 120 477 4100
Email: editorial@ombooks.com
Website: www.ombooksinternational.com

Sales Office
107, Ansari Road, Darya Ganj,
New Delhi 110 002, India
Phone: +91 11 4000 9000
Email: sales@ombooks.com
Website: www.ombooks.com

Copyright © Ravi Shankar Etteth 2025
Illustrations © Ravi Shankar Etteth, developed using AI

ALL RIGHTS RESERVED. No part of this book may be reproduced or transmitted in any form by any means, electronic or mechanical, including photocopying and recording, or by any information storage and retrieval system, except as may be expressly permitted in writing by the publisher.

ISBN: 978-93-6395-064-1

Printed in India

10 9 8 7 6 5 4 3 2 1

To my son Aditya
though more of a limericks guy

CONTENTS

Explanation   xi

1. Secret   1
2. Doll Play   3
3. Serendipity   5
4. Worry   7
5. Revelation   9
6. Bright Child   11
7. Deception   13
8. Zen   15
9. Truth   17
10. You   19
11. So Far So Good   21
12. Last Train Out   23
13. It's Too Late   25
14. Again   27
15. Free Witch   29
16. Daisy Hunter   31
17. Important   33
18. Clean Sweep   35
19. The Vanishing   37
20. Take It Easy   39
21. Good Riddance   41
22. Backfire   43

23.	Autumn	45
24.	Soul Advice	47
25.	Next Morning	49
26.	Scented Day	51
27.	Brother	53
28.	Untamed	55
29.	Vertigo	57
30.	Unwritten Words	59
31.	Martyr	61
32.	Random Roads	63
33.	Last Visitors	67
34.	Remains	69
35.	Precious Detritus	71
36.	At Last	75
37.	Crosswords	77
38.	Last Laugh	79
39.	Wife	81
40.	Loss.com	83
41.	Queen	85
42.	Bazar of the Beloveds	87
43.	Storm	89
44.	Loneliness	93
45.	Matinee of Miracles	95
46.	Tricked	97
47.	Awakening	99
48.	Bones	103
49.	Michelangelo	104
50.	New Airline	106
51.	Confession	109
52.	An Acquired Taste	111
53.	Doubt	113
54.	Dissimulation	115
55.	Time	117
56.	Friendships	118
57.	Eternity	119

Acknowledgements 110

EXPLANATION

I had no intention of ever writing poetry in my life. I saw it as a self-indulgent activity, unless the poets in question were Neruda or Byron. They were more than poets. They were historians of beauty and pain. Ecstasy and revelation. When I came across a poem about a lost soul asking not to be abandoned because she wants to be abandoned, on a whim I wrote a stanza that eventually became this book.

Poetry is about wounds, hurts dressed up as tributes. We don't realize the number of wounds we collect as we carry on through our days and years, or their depth, until we read a good poem. We don't fully see the brightness of sunlight our hearts are blessed with because we are consumed by darkness; ours and others'. In the tide of the years, we float paper boats made from envelopes of old letters, carrying memories of friendships and loneliness, of cigarettes shared and jokes told around a campfire. We venture into unknown horizons, pagan seekers of the soul, learning as we go that not all frontiers are to be crossed, and not all love is redemption. These realms are where poetry takes you. Frees you. Then punishes you.

Poetry is about memories, real and imagined. Have you ever woken from a dream and thought you were actually there? Do you long for that land again? Those are memories you would like to have. The ones you seek. In your memories, you become what you wish to be. You can cheat. Convince yourself something really happened. You can love ghosts who reject you. Poetry is about strangers. People who appear on pages, laughing, sighing, thinking, recounting. When you read, they become real for that moment. They are there to impart a vital essence; a philosophy of revealing and interpreting what something means to you. Often, they unlock a puzzle you have been wrestling with for years.

Still, be careful. The poet, lest they get trapped in the dreams of others. The reader, lest they be seduced by the mirrors in the halls of rhyme, which show not what they wish to be seen as but what they really are.

So, forgive me my trespasses into this vast world of innocence and dark humour. There are short poems, long ones and even a corny one. This book is also an experiment to create a holistic experience with poetry and the allied arts of photography and music. I have tried, with the help of AI, to visually represent my poems with photo-illustrations and composed a playlist of songs which you can access by simply scanning the barcode on the back cover. Imagine, had Rilke a laptop and an Internet connection, would poetry be an app by now? I sincerely hope it doesn't. I hope you find it all deserving of your time.

SECRET

I hoard you in a dark place

Because you're a creature of the night

as is a nightingale.

DOLL PLAY

It fits that it doesn't fit.
Fitting you in you
in the Matryoshka you.
Why nothing fits
is why everything fits.

SERENDIPITY

A poem

looking for a poet

found a girl

looking for a lover

and wrote itself.

WORRY

Every night I fall asleep
knowing you're sleeping safe.
But in my dreams, I'm always awake
fretting about dreams
that won't let you sleep.

REVELATION

I desired you

not because it was you,

but someone else

that was you.

I leave you now

because it is you.

BRIGHT CHILD

She walks alone

wearing a shawl of light.

Afraid, the darkness keeps its distance

but doesn't stop following her.

DECEPTION

You trap me by boring me.

It isn't working.

Behind all the banal chatter

about nasty colleagues, DEI and PC,

hospital visits and busy ambition,

I see you hunting poets.

ZEN

Complete parts

of a broken part.

Clay pot brims over.

TRUTH

In haikus, there are pools, koi,

pebbles and cherry blossoms,

and a subtle mountain.

In you is the poet's heartbreak.

YOU

You is a word

I don't particularly like

because everyone is a you.

Then there is you

whom I particularly like.

And when it is you being you,

I love you.

SO FAR SO GOOD

A chipped wall plate

A small coffee stain on the breakfast counter

An old dog whinnying in its sleep

A blouse flung carelessly on the floor

A brimming vase of chrysanthemums

The strawberry taste of fresh lipstick.

Everything works now,

everything is fine forever.

LAST TRAIN OUT

A poet seeking inspiration

escaped into a pristine poem

to get away from his inspiration.

There he found a lodge and a garden

both as unkempt as his mind.

He took a chair by the fireplace

and found a charred piece of paper

a brown patch of loss.

He decided to write a sonnet.

He did.

The letters were dark and sooty like his beloved's eyes

that spoke to him about old fires.

Afar he heard the hoot of a steam engine,

its rough poetry made him weep.

IT'S TOO LATE

Why did I while springtime away

on false lights, deep wine

and fickle friends

while you were all the seasons

of my heart?

Which I saw as

one wasted summer.

AGAIN

They say some eagles grow old and die.

And some eagles that grow old

fly to a solitary mountain

to find a rock

to crush their beaks on

and pull on their claws

until they fall off.

Then they wait, bleeding, in agony,

until a new beak and new claws grow back

The eagle takes flight renewed.

You are that rock.

FREE WITCH

Michelangelo's little joke
is not Creation, beloved.
It is man asking God not to let go.
Let priests believe
what they like to believe.
I pointed to the glorious height
and told you the truth.
You laughed and left
to dance under the blood moon,
God asking you not to let go.

DAISY HUNTER

I'm in love when I write.
Then I don't like an empty vase on my table.
I went on a stroll, looking
through the meadows of the mind,
and chanced upon something
cold, hard, smooth and shiny
with a tiny, tiny pulse.
I left it behind in the lonely grass
and walked on to pick wild daisies.

IMPORTANT

Birthdays were important.

Anniversaries were not to be missed.

Going to a restaurant, drinking wine and ordering oysters,

looking at each other was important.

So was holding hands,

kissing and sharing a bed.

Now everything is important

except what is important.

CLEAN SWEEP

You are now an empty room in my life

which I'm left with nothing to fill.

On Sunday, between giving the place a good scrub

and taking out the garbage

I misplaced the key.

Don't come back.

Now even you can't get in.

THE VANISHING

How easily we walk,

discarding footsteps on the sand

pretending we are going places.

Skin of my heart

My willing wave

My softest thought

My rare dove

When the tide comes in

the sea will leave no sign

of the route we took,

scoured by a million furrows of loss and longing

that even ancient waters

cannot scrub away.

TAKE IT EASY

That stream is dead.

It rained yesterday,

that's all.

Don't reopen your bag of words.

Nothing grows

on that dead patch.

It feels nothing.

Not even itself.

GOOD RIDDANCE

Your way or the highway

is not a trip we're taking.

No.

We could get separated

on the crowded staircase of wrong ideas,

be trapped in the rush hour of recriminations.

Truth be told, I'm secretly relieved.

As must you be.

I've torn up my ticket but kept the stub

for the sake of old times that never were.

BACKFIRE

The other day

I made a deal with the Devil

to trade my soul for her heart.

The joke is on me because

the deal I made

was with myself.

AUTUMN

Magnolia trees in bloom.

The season changes.

One flower falls

then another

until the earth is a carpet

of red, pink, brown.

He watches them curl and fade.

A new season is here

He writes no more.

SOUL ADVICE

Write

Read

Erase

Remember

Hope

Learn

Weep

Laugh

Leave

NEXT MORNING

A dog barking

A car honking

A hawker shouting out his wares

The smell of fresh chutney.

Oh, forgot you aren't here

The beauty of the ordinary fades.

I make the bed.

SCENTED DAY

There are flowers

that bloom only at night before dying.

Their fragrance perfumes the day.

The gardener dreams

that he is awake.

BROTHER

Going down the rabbit hole of his stories
I reached the adda of the goodbye gods
where he had tarried on the way
to tell them his dreary secrets.
Did he smell the stale incense?
Taste the tepid coffee?
Laugh at the Old Guy's cruel jokes?
He never even left me a note.
A balloon girl is rapping on my window.
The car behind is honking.
I look around,
Scandalized.
Bewildered.
Nosy passengers stare out of bus windows
glad of an opportunity for a gossipy diversion.
The billboards close around me.
The light turns green.
I've just reached myself again
on the fool's errand of mapping his mind
I'm nowhere near home.

UNTAMED

I don't mind waiting.

It is an act I like to observe

in myself,

wondering how long I would last

on that crippled rock

on your sentient shore.

Expecting that one single wave

to slap its hair on the sand

the way you dry your wet hair

after a shower.

Thus, I'll know you have arrived.

I can, then, walk away from the bench

that really belongs to the ocean

of which, you're only some water in the waters.

VERTIGO

You are sick of mind,
sick of body.
When time turns cartwheels
do you get dizzy, or
think life is a circus where
safety nets are scoffed at?
You are sick of mind,
sick of body.
You're your own audience,
and your own fall.

UNWRITTEN WORDS

Carefully

I fold the creamy sheet of paper in four

Fit it neatly in its spotless cream envelope

I don't lick the flap. I glue it down perfectly.

I do lick the postage stamp though.

Sorry,

that is how it is done.

I write your address in black ink

with a calligraphy pen I've been dying to use.

When the postman brings you my letter

which you will open with the heirloom paper knife

I gave you for your birthday ages ago,

don't be puzzled.

The sheet is blank.

I've nothing to say to you,

it's just that I thought of you.

MARTYR

Spare me the dreary disbelief
of your weeping heart.
There has been blood on the water
ever since lovers' smiles played their part.
Those emails you've memorized
the emoticons and calendar dates
Delete
The idle riches of your heart
with not foolishness deplete
Spare me the rusted gratings
of your broken clock which
strikes every mundane hour
with commonplace complaints.
We're not special, you and I.
We're just empty seashells
that echo the ocean's bored sigh.

Stop parenting your mourning

You've nothing unique to prove.

Don't be one of those

who believe their pain is special

and makes them special.

It doesn't

Everyone hurts

They just go on.

RANDOM ROADS

I don't know what this is

I don't know what it can be or won't be

Does this road lead to you or away from you?

Is it the same road by which

my mother waited for her bus

or my father rode his bicycle

to buy fish and fresh flowers?

Is it the road I remember

on which my grandfather strode

with his guns and dogs to shoot white storks

that sailed over green paddy?

And the road on which he was

taken away from me?

My first grief.

It is a road of a million footprints

of people I see, or don't see

and never saw and will ever see

moving to their destinations

today or forever.

It is the road that is you, or perhaps not you

All I know is it is a road

that is yours while you pass by

A road which leads to another road

and another and yet another

until the world is sewn together

by a million journeys.

Yours

Mine

Ours

It is a road by which you cross my path

without a smile of recognition.

A road which isn't there or never was nor will be

A road paved with poems and obituaries

and sliding by temple tarns blessed by ancient, holy trees.

A road with shops

that sold sweet ice and candy to ragamuffins.

A road on which girls walked to school

and thieves slunk along, looking for doors

left carelessly open.

But, it is just a road, beloved,

on which our shadows fell briefly

as the day whittled itself away.

LAST VISITORS

A man in black wearing a hoodie is what I was told.
But it was a woman in white who visited me
in the hospital and gave me a white puppy
which would follow me
through the endless whiteness
I holding her hand.
His hands have black nails I was told.
Her hand was warm, with pretty red nails.
His breath is cold I was told.
Hers smelt of peppermint and fresh apples
as we walked through the endless whiteness,
me holding my puppy close.
His heart is full of black hate I was told.
She stroked my hair softly
wrapped me in her white warm coat
laid me down on a furry rug
and tucked me in safe and warm,
blew me a kiss and walked away.
I held the pup close and watched him come
all dressed in black
with cold hands, black nails and wintry breath.
And she came back with him.

REMAINS

I've scrounged these words for you

from a leftover stanza in a burning book

its stories, a wasted harvest of regrets

watered by the unseasonal monsoon

of hopeful happiness

and the tears of bitter believers.

I am not the clever lover,

a poet of wooing and cunning.

I'm not even a poet

just as you shouldn't be a muse.

Couldn't

Wouldn't

See the stoic words curling in the indifferent flame of

a ten-rupee lighter

The ash of the meanings

of perhaps and maybes

Litter of life

A broken cuckoo clock gone quiet

sandwich scraps, old newspapers

a solitary walk under trees, dreaming in the mist

Silverfish dead in shut-down libraries, torn down

to make way for undistinguished apartments.

Everything is in motion except time

trapped in itself.

My futile last rhyme feels

the impatience in your kindness.

Dusk falls.

PRECIOUS DETRITUS

The curtains are drawn

Sheets cover the furniture

Doors and windows locked

Bags packed

The key is in the usual place.

Do you mind stopping by

to pick up the book we used to read together?

The book that began

'It was the best of times, it was the worst of times,

it was the age of wisdom,

it was the age of foolishness,

it was the epoch of belief,

it was the epoch of incredulity,

it was the season of light, it was the season of darkness,

it was the spring of hope, it was the winter of despair.'

We never got beyond that

how many ever times we picked it up.

You and I, we're done

but a part of me will always love you.

We're all stocked with such odds and ends.

That bittersweet thing we call love

is the best part of us which stays back

long after the last bus has left.

AT LAST

The wind in the heart

is at last quiet.

Your sigh makes the hour shiver.

A leafless plant with just one flower.

Pick it on your way out.

CROSSWORDS

It's Sunday, beloved.

You're asleep again

already having forgotten

you lay in my arms all night.

I open the newspaper and reach for my pencil.

The crossword puzzle

is a game of black and white,

which is anything but.

Every white square I fill

with letters of your name

until I have so many names for you

Euphonious

fantastical

brittle

tongue twisting

nonsensical.
They are all your names, nameless one.
The only name that makes sense to me.
And I know you're a puzzle
you think you've solved yourself.
I shake my head smiling
and put the newspaper away
on a shelf in my room which is crowded
with thousands of Sundays and crosswords
all bearing your name.
I get back into bed
which is still warm with you
take you back in my arms
smell the night in your hair
and hold you close
and closer because I know
you will never be there,
beloved of delusions, till next Sunday
when you'll be sleeping in our bed again.

LAST LAUGH

When I reached the passport office today
I heard much wailing and keening
with breakwaters of stoic silences
in between rough waves of rage
and spindrift of explanations
I saw brochures of heartbreak
shredded into official confetti.
The clerk at the window looked at me
competently, curiously,
as if thinking, This guy? Seriously?
I opened my brand-new passport
smelt its virgin paper
and touched the unmarked pages
and your photograph stared out at me.
The clerk sniggered smugly,
'The government has a new rule.
Now, passport pictures will be of the person who
broke your heart.'
They got it wrong.
It was I who broke her heart.
Typical bureaucrats.

WIFE

If I lean you against the tree of life
on the soft slope of this misty hill
where my breath pools around you
like a lost explorer's cloak
will you tell me why
I cannot kiss the world away.
If I hold your pale fingers
as I would hold a solemn promise
and scrape its nails along my cheek,
leaving a precious scar in this abandoned hour,
will you tell me why
I cannot take back the cloudy day.
Why you came back to me without
the white shroud I wrapped you in.
The pines stand straight and stoic
with the solemnity that marks new widowers.
We had walked these little mountain roads
collected pinecones and picnicked
in the woods of longing.

I ate buttered scones off your mouth

laid you down on the soft wild grass

and wrapped your pale body with the sunset.

I still keep your generous heat

wrapped in tattered kerchiefs of marooned memory.

Will you tell me why

when I lean you against the tree of life again

I feel cold and uncertain

like rain without a sky.

LOSS.COM

I knew you would steal in with stealthy pride
to this light-speckled hall of deceitful nuances,
chandeliers, champagne, cliques and conversations,
with your awkward wide-hipped gait
diacriticals of disquiet on your pallid forehead
deviously dispassionate, yet curious
to know if pleasant distance has changed me
from a sitient butterfly into a malevolent moth
whose velvet dust poisons irrelevant desire
that dies every day on the soul's blades of grass.
I see you consolidating your habit of being you,
a branch without a swing, a bird without a wing,
a painting without a painter, a curse without a god,
a kite without destiny, pain without a wound.
Leave, you soul without substance,
back to your haunted museum of emotional artefacts,
of fear, twisted memories and salty loneliness,
empty without the redemption of guilt.
No coveted coupon of intimacy for you,
I have moved to a different city
of lips, breasts, swirling navel and cloudy hair
from where sometimes I write you
emails which I send to me.

QUEEN

After the war,

fleeing through the ruined gates

of her heart's complications,

she finds herself in a city of grieving ghosts,

fathers and sons, kings and princes,

nameless messengers and careless spies

all scythed down

in the illicit appetency of a fallen monarch

and the spendthrift vengeance of a sacred bow.

She crosses the fateful fields

of homecoming

acknowledging the lament of the neighbourhood sea

whose waves froth crimson and black,

roaring like wounded warhorses in their last charge.

The drums are quiet on the battlefield of metaphors,

soaked in the splendid blood

of an austere author's mind

where warriors had perished

for a glimpse of her unbound hair

She recalls the enchanted chariot of the sky,

now ownerless and unyoked,

remembers touching cotton-candy clouds,

soft and subtle like the volume of loving phantoms,

and the musky warrant of her abductor's desire

seducing her to savour sensuous solitude.

She longs for the garden

where she had spent

life's happiest years

as her own hostage.

BAZAR OF THE BELOVEDS

There is a new day of the week

An eighth one

like a glass sheet slid by time

between solitary weekends.

It is the day of the Bazar of the Beloveds

where dreams are purveyed

in the black market of desires

where romantic revenants seek a bargain,

their currency, greed, or despair.

Let them take their pick.

Soiled love letters bleeding passion

like pomegranates ripened in a summer of sighs

pawned wedding rings

pink cell phones that ring no more

torn Valentine cards

little vials filled with the strychnine of goodbyes

scented handkerchiefs

mementos of sunny days and sweet sweat

a faded rose but with thorn intact

that had touched lovelorn blood of departed joys.

I knew I would run into you here.

Thief of my heart I have things to do,

thoughts to bury, needs to hide, plans to make,

and secrets to hoard.

I have no need for pilfered heartbeats

bargained for and bought in the Bazar of the Beloveds

which stays hidden between our lost days

when your body was the bridge

between then and now.

STORM

The death of what we had dazzles me
The sky within flashes so bright I cannot see
A ship plunges into a great wave's trough within
As I remember how I loved you with storm and skin
How high it rises
to meet the waters hurled at me.
I, exulting in thunder, the surf, and all the melee,
a mariner braving dark tides of the heart,
sailing into wild weather, playing the part,
believing that you mattered to me forever,
knowing you won't occur to me again or ever.
as you did once.
And how it burns.
How does something I had breathed as air
now is as if it was never even there.
Can I have back the words I gave you to keep
before I go back into the light, return to the deep?

Wait, there's a raindrop on your eyelash
I'll whisper and watch it softly splash
on the cobblestones of this never-ending road
Which evasion's million steps cannot corrode.
The death of what we had dazzles me
I never knew freedom is so powerful.

LONELINESS

What you see as my mask,

you fool,

is my face.

You'll be blinded if you see my mask

of thorns, blood and excrement of wolves.

Don't be misled by my voice

sweetly poisoned with tongues of dead songbirds

and glazed with a harsh orchestra of crows

singing psalms of a stand-up guy

bleeding on a scaffold.

I'm not your god

or anyone's god for that matter

I'm my own god

and I want you.

MATINEE OF MIRACLES

I got tickets

to the matinee of miracles.

I thought of driving you in a gleaming big car,

opening the door gallantly

stopping at the fancy restaurant where they

bow and scrape each time I enter.

I'm a big tipper.

You have a shy smile and bright eyes.

I thought of sitting with you in the last row,

linking hands and eating popcorn of the soul

sipping colas and stealing wanton kisses.

Just before the curtain rose I figured

you are the star of the show

which is I.

TRICKED

You are a gift

to be unwrapped slowly,

breathlessly.

Does a gift lose hope and magic

once it is opened?

Or does it presage more gifts

like walking hand in hand

with you by the Ganga,

or watching you stir sugar in your morning coffee,

or the kiss you blow before getting into your cab,

which were gifts even before they were gifts?

A gift that enchants the most desolate recipient

who believes it is his gift, and his alone to unwrap

until he discovers it is an empty box

which he and only he can fill.

AWAKENING

Four hundred million souls and more
in the greatest Instagram show in the world
to be seen and heard by man and god.
Dip, baby, dip.
A time of great churning, pyres for demons
squirming and screaming in the fire of gods.
Salvation point where the three rivers meet
on the sandy shore of the City of Bliss.
Influencers and instagrammers,
silver screen stars and social media mavens,
photographers and painters,
socialites and socialists, kitty-party wives
and tequila tots, CEOs and clerks,
grocers and cab drivers, fashionistas and bureacrats,
politicians and pilers-on, dhobis and doctors,

beggars and bystanders

Sinners and shopkeepers, priests and peons,

ascetics fierce and naked, charlatans and champions,

pickpockets and pundits

in the greatest Instagram show in the world.

Dip, baby, dip.

Redemption meets immortality

sin gets a 'Get Out of Jail Free' card

virtue glows eternal

the Sacred Feminine

loved and choked, prayed to and poisoned,

worshipped and violated.

She, the numinous patroness of an ancient land

of blessed brightness and daily darkness

on the immortal canvas of contradictions.

Dip, baby, dip.

iPhone cameras wink, sirens scream and

power flashes by with sirens, red lights and policemen.

Scrap and shit, death in the mud,

screams and salutations, tents aflame,

in the greatest Instagram show in the world.

A heartstopping time, a pulse-ripping time

of VIP passes and bus tickets,

the holy riviera, or railway station hotels

it doesn't matter where

in the greatest Instagram show in the world.

Faith is the only ticket of the soul

to sold-out heaven.

Dip, baby, dip.

Beyond a bend in the river

where stone steps lead to the water as they had

in the age when good and evil fought

and the water became nectar

a mother bathes.

She tells her little boy to come into the water.

He is cold, he pleads, and that god will understand.

A little temple bell piggybacks on the wind

the mother coaxes with jalebis

the child hesitates, grins and hops down

to wriggle his toe in the water.

In a tiny temple on the ridge above

neither important nor magnificent,

not the stuff of travel brochures

nor hallowed by tenacious tourist touts

a small stone lamp comes to flame.

The boy yields and enters the water

with a shiver and squeals of laughter

and splashes water on his mother.

God sees, hears and smiles

now awake.

BONES

Bones of little children scattered everywhere
Sobibor, Kibbutz Be'eri, Gaza, Somalia, Syria
Bones so shredded you cannot put together even
with a 3D printer to see how the kid looked like.
Bones that stink of cordite, burned microwave,
gasoline, hummus and candy.
If you look closely you will find names scribbled
on little femurs, hip bones, pieces of skulls,
tiny patterns and spiky shapes made by drones
and missiles, bombs and cars.
Meanwhile. elegant men and women
drink champagne on art-decco terraces
overlooking pretty lakes, and talk about the next
dinner in Davos and the New York Stock Exchange.
Bones are not conversations
Bones are no fun
Bones don't make people rich unless you're one
of those wearing a keffiyeh in luxurious exile,
or dudes in tuxes selling sarin to demented dictators.
Something from the darkness comes from time to
time to pick up the pieces of little children and
take them away to the crypts of collective amnesia
to make us forget
again and again.

MICHELANGELO

In the ancient city of Firenze
there's a piazza presided over
by the Church of Santa Croce
where Galileo and Michelangelo doze in their crypts.
There are cafés in the square
which serve wine in large flasks.
I poured a glass of Chianti
lit a cigar and noticed that the wine
was redder than your lips,
but only slightly.
This is a memory of something that never happened,
of you gripping my hand fiercely
when we suddenly came upon David rising
like a great white miracle of marble
even straight men would lust after.

You stared fiercely at the Tree of Life
and turned to fix your great dark eyes on mine.
Your gasp smelt of mint.
I don't know where you went.
I called you from Rome airport but you didn't answer,
probably trapped in little Excels cells at a business meeting
or drinking whisky, not Chianti, with your after-work friends
or exploring the tongue of a new lover
lost in forgotten sensations.
I find a bar, order a Jameson which I don't particularly like
but suited the mood
and looked for my carry on
when a strange woman's voice called my flight number.
I woke up,
dog hair on my bed
and sunlight sliding in through the blinds,
and wondered if Michelangelo and Galileo could
pull off the star of a woman
whom I will always recognize, even in death,
because she is you.
So I burned all art in my gallery of hope.
Please pick up the phone.

NEW AIRLINE

I was on my way to a conference in another city

I chose this new airline everybody is talking about

Deep seats, gourmet food, vintage wines,

Madhubala meets Gal Gadot stewardesses.

Tickets cheaper than a coquette's wink

There's a catch though.

Passengers can't look at each other

Get caught on CCTV you'll be flown back.

I sank into my plush seat,

heard silk subtly moving close-by

on skin softer than a lover's scented breath.
I became aware of her in the window seat
sensed the air tracing the line of that perfect nose
the shifting waterfall of her hair.
I felt her like a wind smelling flowers
I felt the heat of her like an ember in a fireplace
I closed my eyes to life flowing through the length of her
and pour through the swirling roots of her soul
I turned my head and pretended to look out
at the clouds suspended in the blue outside
and her eyes met mine, scorching my heart.
Her nose pin flung sunfire into my eyes.
Her mouth was redder than I imagined,
bruised carnations and strawberry candy.
A smile shivering at the corner of her lower lip
keeping in eddies of kisses.
They were waiting at the airport to send us home.
It's been a while now
By now I'm out of air miles
But I'm afraid to miss my flight
On the airline of Never Never land.

CONFESSION

Midnight steps

on the shore of revelations

at the moment the last wave

of the day's last hour

spends itself on the sand

you pick up a sea shell and whisper,

'Darling, listen to the sea within,

it is the sound of eternity.'

I take it from you just as the first wave

of the next day comes ashore

and throws it into the shriven wind

and tell you the secret why trees grow,

fish swim and pine cones fall in the wind.

'Beloved, listen to the sea, not to its ghost.'

Let us stop haunting ourselves.

AN ACQUIRED TASTE

Once when I was young and bold
I kissed a girl in a seaside town
and melted in her tender tide
of smoky spice, warm chocolate
and cigarette smoke which often
flavour the seasons of my life,
unspoken, unforgotten.
It's a different place now, a different time.
Memory in denial.
She now feels uncomfortable.
Protestations that make no sense.
It hardly matters.
My heart will always return to swim
in the lost age of an endless kiss,
a shark tamed by tongue and lip
Though I knew long ago
it wasn't her I was holding on to
It's her kiss I cannot let go.

DOUBT

You complained that I loved you

with that special moue of yours

gathering your thick brows

that look like rainclouds in a bad mood.

I confess it was a charming infatuation

like wanting to keep a kitten

that had strayed into the kitchen and purred

when fed condensed milk in a porcelain bowl.

Wait.

I do not do you justice

Not a kitten

a cheetah, maybe

But your claws have left marks

which I cannot locate

but hurts enough to make me wonder

if it was just an infatuation at all.

DISSIMULATION

'We are what we are.'

Nonsense.

'But this isn't the real me.'

Nonsense.

We destroy ourselves

defending what we have become

at the hands of others.

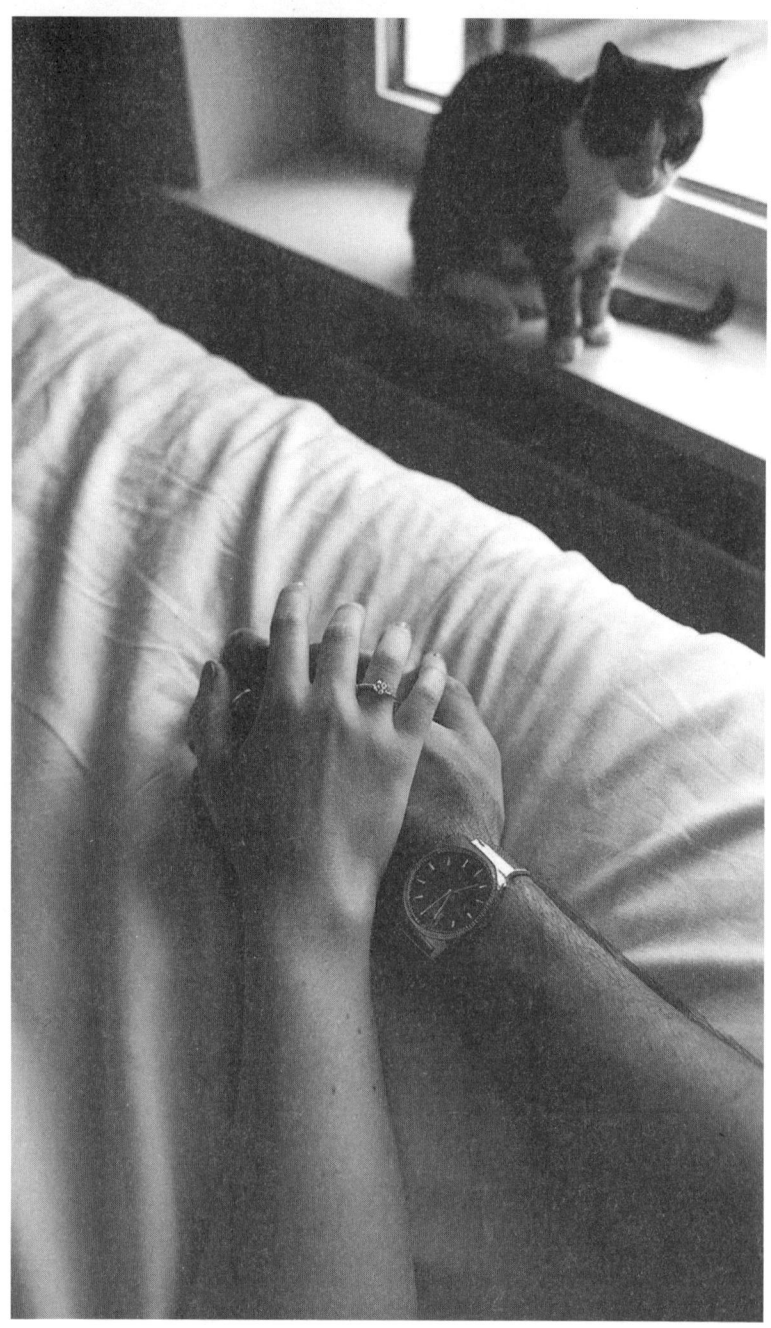

TIME

Was I not enough

for you to love me

when you desired me?

We've risen, we've set

Isn't that enough?

I waited for you

with wine, music and witticisms

and dervishes to dance with

on the patient meadow of serendipity.

Now that my time

is circling the clock

why didn't you tell me

you were with me all along?

FRIENDSHIPS

These hide-and-seek conversations

The measured silences and ambush of words

enigmas and entreaties.

Stop.

Instead

let's talk of newspapers and ice cream

of EVs, world peace and zardozi

Karan Johar, Gaza and snowy mountains.

Then

Look for spaces between words.

Maybe they mean nothing.

Who knows

nothing has the power to be something.

Sometimes.

ETERNITY

The wave is bored

The rock has sunk

On the beach

a pebble remembers.

ACKNOWLEDGEMENTS

To my editor Shantanu who obviously saw in me something I didn't, my agent Lipika who persuaded me that these poems must be published, Shampa Kamath whose edits and suggestions were invaluable as usual, Anika and Anish Mohla for excellent feedback and help in choosing the music, tech wizard Magesh for advice on AI, and Mishti Bose for her Bacchanalian contribution.